STUTT
A Gu
in a F

Written and illustrated by Daniele Rossi

Special thanks for proofing
and critiquing my very first book:

Annie Bradberry
Connie Crosby
Christine Dits
Samuel Dunsiger
Mandy Finstad
Jane Lebak
Grant Meredith
Kiara Mavalwala
Melanie and Nate Rogers
Greg Snyder
Claire Falcon Tan

© 2014 Daniele Rossi All rights reserved. Reproduction of this book, including the cartoon characters, comics and plots, in any form is strictly prohibited without the express written permission of Daniele Rossi. Except in the case of a reviewer who wishes to quote in brief passages for the sake of a review written for inclusion in a magazine, newspaper, journal, blog or other form of online and offline publication. Contact Daniele at daniele@stutteringiscool.com. Any plots in the comics, including situations depicted, are strictly coincidental. Should any of these resemble your life, well, like I said, it's coincidental. But hey, that means you can boast that your life is perfect for comics!

The information in this book is for educational purposes only and is based on my own personal experiences with stuttering. I am not a speech pathologist, I'm just a person who stutters with experience in gaining confidence by facing fears of stuttering openly.

℗ 2014 ISBN 978-0-9921632-0-4

MISCHIEF,
MAYHEM
AND MIRTH
PUBLISHING

"I ♥ MY STUTTERER"

"BEING A PERSON WHO STUTTERS HAS BEEN A HARD PATH AT TIMES but it has made me STRONGER & wiser"

"STUTTERING HAS VALUE... SINCE OPENING UP ABOUT MY STUTTERING MY WORLD HAS OPENED UP PROFOUNDLY AND DEEPLY"

"YOU ARE UNIQUE you didn't choose STUTTERING yet you've been chosen to figure out HOW TO FIND MEANING IN YOUR LIFE in spite of stuttering. Remember, STUTTERING MAKES YOU MUCH MORE INTERESTING than all those average people who are fluent."

"There's a difference between knowing THERE ARE OTHER PEOPLE who stutter out there & MEETING THEM"

"WE ALL HAVE THE INNATE ABILITY TO REACH DOWN DEEP TO OVERCOME - JUST ABOUT ANY CHALLENGE THROWN OUR WAY"

"TO FIND ACCEPTANCE OF OUR STUTTERING WE MUST FIRST CHIP AWAY AT THE negative feelings and attitudes dragging us down such as shame, embarrassment and guilt"

"CONTROL IT Do not let it control you"

" Improving one's stutter is like playing guitar. When you first learn a song, you will never play it smoothly. Over time, with enough practice, you will eventually become fluent with the song and produce great music. "

"DON'T LET THE ELEPHANT IN THE ROOM be a shameful elephant"

"STUTTERING is neither GOOD OR BAD. It just is."

"I really value and admire people's ability to be vulnerable and be open and let their guard down which is a very difficult, courageous thing to do in today's society."

" So much of stuttering is the way you think about it "

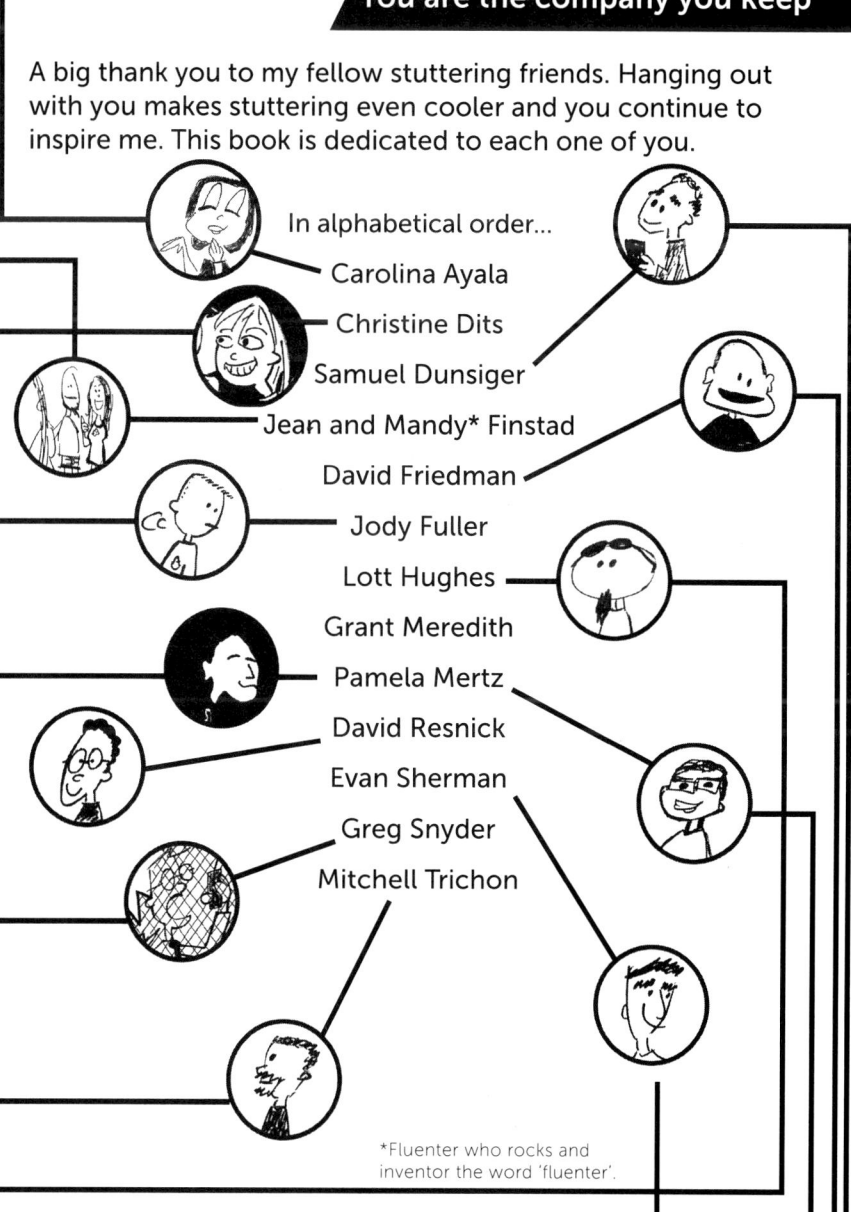

You are the company you keep

A big thank you to my fellow stuttering friends. Hanging out with you makes stuttering even cooler and you continue to inspire me. This book is dedicated to each one of you.

In alphabetical order...

Carolina Ayala

Christine Dits

Samuel Dunsiger

Jean and Mandy* Finstad

David Friedman

Jody Fuller

Lott Hughes

Grant Meredith

Pamela Mertz

David Resnick

Evan Sherman

Greg Snyder

Mitchell Trichon

*Fluenter who rocks and inventor the word 'fluenter'.

WHAT'S YOUR NAME?

by Daniele Rossi

Introducing Franky Banky, protagonist of this book's comics.

Stuttering will not limit you unless you want it to

I stuttered since I was four years old* but didn't notice anything out of the ordinary until I was about seven when other kids began to point it out in a negative way. So I learned at a very early age that the way I talked was "wrong" and I grew to become afraid of stuttering every time I spoke. Stuttering tends to be regarded as something "bad" because it isn't "normal" and because of the negative feedback those of us who stutter get from other people who are jerks or may not know what stuttering is.

We live in a society that expects perfection and looks down upon weakness despite the fact that humans are never, ever perfect. From air brushed celebrities on magazines to scripted "reality" TV, our society is focused way too much on desperately trying to appear perfect and "be like everybody else". Humans are social beings after all. It's natural that we want to fit in.

Since stuttering is easily regarded as bad, we go through life trying to pass ourselves off as fluent. We switch words, pretend to forget what we were going to say, describe the places where we live instead of saying the name, order food we really don't want, give fake names instead of our own, or mess up or miss out on social situations and not be ourselves. This, in turn, can wreak havoc with our sense of self-worth.

We are the same normal, regular human beings as those who are fluent, blind, use wheelchairs, hard of hearing, tall, short, fat, skinny, muscular, blonde, brunette, redhead, wear glasses, etc. Everyone has their strengths and weaknesses in any number of areas. There will always be someone in the world who is better than us at something. Just because it can suck to stutter doesn't mean it has to control us.

We need to be proactive. This is what this book is all about. Besides, stuttering allows us to quickly find out which people make better friends.

*I was also the only one in my family who stuttered. In fact, I didn't know anyone else who stuttered until my mid-30s.

Like I said, I stuttered since I was about 4 years old back in the 1970s when disco was all the rage long before the Internet and social media came to be. In those days, it tended to be difficult to meet another person who stutterers in your immediate geographical area. You pretty much experienced stuttering alone.

Me back then

I was embarrassed by my stuttering and tried to hide it as much as possible

Using tricks to fool others into saying the words for me

But this only made me look like I lacked the smarts to form sentences

Switched words I was really going to say

Most times this placed me into more socially awkward situations as I ran out of words to substitute

Feared and avoided a number of social situations

Never an advantage

Worst of all, I stayed silent at times

Never, ever an advantage

All this because of the negative feedback I got from interacting with people who don't stutter (I'll call them "fluenters" going forward).

Odd, isn't it? It was as if stuttering was my fault.

Me now (2007 and on)

No longer embarrassed by my stuttering and I'm enjoying the benefits of not hiding it

I'm no longer resorting to tricks

I get to say what I want to say and just be myself

No longer switching words.

This helps me learn which words I need to work on and choose the right tool for saying them

Social situations are a lot more fun when the people I meet know I am totally cool about my stuttering

I no longer remain silent. People can't shut me up!

By having met confident stutterers, I learned about acceptance and the benefits of stuttering openly and feeling at ease.

Despite what research continues to reveal, I still meet many people who believe in the misinformation they read online about stuttering, blame everything on their stuttering, believe they will never amount to anything because of their stuttering, and that stuttering is their fault.

I'm sharing with you in this book what worked for me and the fellow stuttering friends I've met since launching my podcast* in 2007.

*stutteringiscool.com

Wait... Hold it.
Did I just introduce myself
by only talking about my stuttering?

What was I thinking?

Stuttering isn't everything!

intensely creative individual

likes to try new things

a visual person

likes comedies

still listens to shortwave radio

armchair astronomer

animation enthusiast

cat person (I like dogs, too)

appreciation for slapstick

enjoys cooking

Me

reads newspaper comics

weakness for blue cheese

enjoys going on adventures

appreciates art

loooooooooves music

listens to old time radio

a little obsessed with working out

enjoys helping people

a little impatient

enjoys cartooning

actually enjoys shovelling snow

and I happen to stutter.

Sure my stuttering experience shaped me into the person
I am but there is so much more to us stutterers than
stuttering.

f-f-f-f-f-f... f-f-f-f-f... f-f-f-f-... f-f-f-f-four-four

As you know, unless you're a fluenter reading this (yay!), stuttering occurs when you are about to say something you want to say but for neurological reasons, your body won't let you say it for a few seconds or even a few minutes. Stuttering can be in the form of r-r-r-r-repetitions, prrrroooooollllllooooongations and/or b... b... b... blocks (also known as 'gestural fixations'). We try to get control of our mouths back but our bodies just won't let us. To accommodate, we move other body parts like stamping our feet, blinking, or losing eye contact. This is our body's attempt at getting ready to say the next sound we are trying to say. All this has nothing to do with us sounding different. Anyone would be anxious about this regardless of speech fluency. Generally, fluenters have no knowledge about all this so they do nutty things like look at us funny, try to finish our sentences, or give us bad grades in school. This is why stuttering tends to feel bad. And as humans, regardless of our speech, we tend to focus on our negative experiences rather than our positives like our strengths and the people in our lives who see past our stuttering.

**Keep calm
and
stammer on**

Stuttering is not an indication of intelligence level.
Get over it.

Stuttering is not an indication of
or caused by fear or anxiety.
Get over it.

Stuttering is not an indication of poor character.
Get over it.

Stuttering is not your or your parents' fault.
Accept it.

Your life won't change even if you magically
stopped stuttering right now.
Accept it.

And there is always someone worse off than you.
Remember this.

ffffffffffffffffffiiiiiiiiiiiiiiive

How I went from "Me Back Then" to

"Me Now (2007 and on)"

It was 2006 and I was still in a job that I didn't like. I shopped around for a speech pathologist as it had been a few decades since I've had speech therapy. However, I couldn't shake off the feeling that I needed something more. But I didn't know what.

SOMETHING NEEDS TO CHANGE

EITHER MY STUTTERING GOES AWAY...

OR I DO SOMETHING ABOUT IT

I started attending podcasting conferences the following year. By June, I began to get the hang of networking but I was still self-conscious about stuttering so I wasn't quite victorious at it.

I'VE HAD SPEECH THERAPY MANY TIMES BEFORE BUT... I DON'T KNOW... I JUST DON'T... KNOW... BUT I NEED TO GO ON JOB INTERVIEWS...

In the meantime, I started producing a podcast about creativity called *SpudCast*. I spent hours and hours re-recording episodes every time I stuttered. I also spent a good three hours editing my stuttering out. I always felt like I was being dishonest to my listeners but I couldn't figure out why. I couldn't stutter on the air, could I?

I still don't know how it happened, but out of the blue in September...

I WISH I COULD MEET ALL THESE PEOPLE

I recorded an off topic episode all about my stuttering. I shared how I didn't know what caused it but I knew for certain that it had nothing to do with low self-confidence or being afraid.

Maybe I felt safe because I didn't have many listeners!

After posting the episode, I tried a search for stuttering podcasts. I did this every-so-often but only forums with people complaining about stuttering came up.

Back in 2005, a podcast called *StutterCast* popped up. While the host stuttered, he didn't talk about stuttering and he stopped podcasting after a while. This time around, *StutterTalk* came up with eleven episodes. It had three co-hosts at the time and one of the hosts, Greg Snyder, stood out to me.

I remember him talking about how stuttering just is and it's not our fault. I learned that speech therapy isn't a cure as I thought it was supposed to be and it's better to stutter openly.

This was also the first time I heard about stuttering support groups. And friends stuttering openly together in public places to practice their speech therapy.

The concept of having friends who also stuttered totally appealed to me.

This was that void that I needed filling. Speech therapy wasn't enough. I needed to meet other people who stutter. I also found listening to other people stutter like me on *StutterTalk* comforting and therapeutic. I didn't care what they were talking about as long as they were stuttering! So I started my search for support groups where I live in Toronto, Canada.

I couldn't find any.

D-D-D-DARN

But I was determined. Since I was already deep in podcasting culture, it was inevitable and only natural that I thought of podcasting.

A PODCAST WHERE LISTENERS CAN SEND RECORDINGS OF THEMSELVES STUTTERING...

I PLAY THEM ON MY SHOW SO WE ALL HEAR EACH OTHER STUTTERING...

MEH... THIS WON'T LAST 4 EPISODES

WHO'S GOING TO RECORD THEMSELVES STUTTERING?

I'LL STILL GIVE IT A TRY. WHAT HAVE I GOT TO LOSE?

It felt good not to re-record or edit my stuttering. To my surprise, it did last beyond four episodes and ended up overshadowing *SpudCast*.

I received a lot of positive feedback towards my stuttering at the podcasting conferences when I told people what my podcast was about. This helped me tremendously with replacing my old covert and negative perspective towards stuttering with a new, positive, and proactive approach.

Through my podcast and the online community I created around it, I made friends with others who stuttered just like me all over the world. Including becoming good friends with Greg. I learned so much from my friends and listeners.

Though I've built my own websites since 56k modems were the bee's knees, it wasn't until I began interacting with the community around my new *Stuttering is Cool* podcast when I realized how much Internet technology helps us help others around the world who share our unique experiences. Without having to meet them in person first (that usually happens after).

I came home one Saturday night at 1 a.m. sometime in 2008. Because I'm a geek, I turned on my computer. My instant messaging program was running and one of my listeners in Alberta, Canada, contacted me. He was in first year post-secondary school and told me that he was nervous about having to give an oral presentation in front of his class the following week. I gave him advice, shared stories from my own experience and then the topic eventually lead to girls and stuttering. After I logged off an hour later, I suddenly realized the significance of what just happened.

My listener was across the country in a different time zone. We never met in person. One stutterer was helping another stutterer. Over instant messaging. Above and beyond speech therapy. With the advent of affordable computers, Internet access, recording gear, web hosting, and free software requiring little or no technical knowledge, mentorship between people who stutter can now transcend geographical boundaries. It's no longer a rarity to meet someone else who stutters online. I've made contact with listeners in areas with no speech therapists or even a word for stuttering!

It came time to check out the legendary National Stuttering Association (NSA) conference that I heard so much about.

That happened in 2010. But more on that later.

nnnnnnnnniiiiiiiiiiiine

I played this mental game in many situations as I grew up: striking up conversations, speaking up in meetings at work, asking strangers for the time, etc. I regretted it each time I let my fear get the best of me. Humans are wired to use fear as a means to survive and stay alive. But fear can also work against us. Staying within your comfort zone prevents you from finding out how strong you are and how much people really don't care about your stuttering.

t<long, awkward pause>en

Bodily functions are also necessary for our survival! But my message here is that even those who don't stutter break wind just like us. We're normal just like everybody else.

Those tricks I listed back at the beginning of the book? It's actually worse when you rely on them. Sure you're "almost fluent" but you're always in a panic. Those new words you start to use in place of others? You will evetually end up stuttering on them, too.

Make a pledge to yourself not to switch words and take the baby steps you need to face your fears one speaking situation at a time. You will grow into a confident and overt, person who stutters. And celebrate your victories no matter the size. Inform the uninformed and enjoy your life by pursuing your passions. Not everyone will give you negative feedback. So give yourself the chance to get that positive feedback.

I went nightclubbing a lot in my 20s and I liked the fact that I didn't stutter as I shouted over the loud music. This comic continues on the next page.

el-l-l... el-l-l... el-l-l... el-l-l... el-l-l... el-l-l... even

At the same time, I didn't like the fact that I had to shout every time I wanted to talk. It hurt my throat and you can't say much anyway. Me: HOW. DO. YOU. LIKE. THE. DJ? She: WHAT? Me: HOW. DO. YOU. LIKE. THE. DJ? She: WHAT? Me: DO. YOU. WANT. TO. GO. GET. A. DRINK? She: WHAT? Me: DO. YOU. WANT. TO. GO. GET. A. DRINK? She: NO. THIS. IS. MY. FIRST. TIME. COMING. HERE.

tw... tw... tw... tw... e... elve

10 benefits of stuttering (in no particular order)

We had a topic in a Stutter Social* hangout one night where we asked participants to each mention a benefit of stuttering. Despite the initial shock of such a radical question, it turned out that it wasn't very hard to build the list. In no particular order:

1. In general, stuttering makes us compassionate and can give us a sense of empathy for other people and their issues.

2. It allows us to meet inspiring people from around the world and share our experiences with them.

3. It lets us overcome obstacles and challenges that even fluent people may be afraid of doing, such as public speaking.

4. It gives us a sense of persistence and dedication to being the best person that we can be.

5. It makes us memorable. It's an interesting, exciting trait!

6. Stuttering makes us prioritize and achieve our goals like practicing our speech tools, improving our fitness, following our passions, etc.

7. As people who stutter, learning how to deal with problems makes us feel more liberated.

8. Stuttering gives us a sense of discipline.

9. Stuttering can open up career paths by pursuing a rewarding career in your passion. Or how about helping people as a career in speech language pathology?

10. Stuttering teaches us how to get our message across effectively. Or to put it another way, fluency isn't the key to getting your message across effectively.

*In 2011, I was asked to co-found Stutter Social, an online community using group video chats to connect people who stutter.

th-th-th-th-th-th-th-th-th-th-th-th-th-th-th... th-th-th-th-th-th-irteen

SOUNDS LIKE THIS B-BOOK IS SUGGESTING TH-THAT I...GASP! S-STUTTER O-O-OPENLY

ARE YOU CRAZY, BOOK?!

No. Just a fan of taking baby steps to overcome a fear.

Operation: Baby Steps

Taking baby steps is the best way to move out of your comfort zone. Perform a small act of courage one day or situation at a time.

For instance, telling a friend that you stutter, phoning up a store to ask for business hours, walking into a store and stutter, or joining a Toastmasters group in your area. You will immediately feel less afraid of stuttering openly after doing each act of courage.

If you feel nervous about trying certain small acts of courage, ask a friend to accompany you. But try not to rely on your friends too much or else they will become a crutch. Your goal here is to grow comfortable with stuttering in front of strangers and you won't have your friend with you in every speaking situation.

Don't forget to celebrate your accomplishments no matter how small!

LET's PLAY NOPE NOPE BINGO!

PUT YOURSELF IN AS MANY SPEAKING SITUATIONS AS YOU CAN.
SEE HOW MANY TIMES YOU GET NEGATIVE FEEDBACK.
KEEP GOING UNTIL YOU GET POSITIVE FEEDBACK. THAT'S 1 POINT.
REPEAT UNTIL DESIRED NUMBER OF POSITIVE FEEDBACK.
(SPOILER ALERT. YOU'LL HAVE MORE POSITIVE THAN NEGATIVE, I BET)

D-D-D-Do Y-Y-You H-H-H-HAVE TH-THESE IN S-S-S-S-SIZE F-F-F-F...

NOPE

A TICK-TICK-TICK-TICK-TICKET...

NOPE

FR-FR-FR-FR-FR-FR-FR-FR-FR-FR-FR-FR-FR...

PATIENT, POLITELY SMILING

BINGO!

PLAY WITH YOUR STUTTERING FRIENDS!

HEE HEE HEE HEE HEE HEE

DID YOU SEE THE CONFUSED LOOK ON HER FACE? HA HA HA HA HA HA HA HA HA HA

The Ti-Ger Analogy of Stuttering Empowerment

In 2010, my friend Greg Snyder, who is a stuttering research scientist and fellow stutterer, saw an analogy of stuttering avoidance vs. empowerment while playing with baby tigers in the zoo.

He noticed he got pounced on every time he turned his back on a baby tiger. This analogy inspired me so much that I created a cartoon tiger and named it Ti-Ger. Get it? It's a block!

I shared my new cartoon with my stuttering friends on Twitter and the next thing I knew, they all began to buy stuffed toy tigers to keep as mascots at their workplaces!

Let's say we have a ferocious tiger that represents our stuttering. Your tiger and your stuttering are one and the same. We can try to lock that tiger in a closet but he's too powerful for the door so he bursts through it. The tiger is able to escape whenever it wants. And when it exits its closet, he will pounce on you, tear you up and ruthlessly kick your butt.

It won't work if you try to deal with this ferocious tiger by turning your back on him. He'll continue to kick your butt. You think to yourself *Tiger's not there — OW! Tiger's not there — OW!* Denial of stuttering does not work. Covering up your stutter doesn't seem to work either.

So you turn to face the tiger. It's a frightening process but you confront him. And you may get beat down at first, but you don't let that tiger make your decisions.

Slowly, your tiger begins to lose its power over you, and you begin to experience more peace and control over your life. You may even get into voluntary stuttering, which is a reversal of power.

Acceptance is not the same as giving up

You don't have to give up on speech tools or speech therapy

<holding up hands and toes trying to denote 16> OW! Ok, sssssixteen.

Stuttering used to make you afraid of talking and feel like a failure of communication. But as your tiger gets weaker, you get to that point that you're more in control of yourself and your speech.

You now have the tiger on a leash and you walk around town; your fear of stuttering and social punishment is now minimal. You may even go up to people and voluntarily stutter! *Hey! Do you wanna see my tiger?* And you reach a point where you're actually ok with it.

And you start showing him off. And you take the tiger back off the leash and you're petting him.

When you face the animal, the animal can back down. When you face stuttering, it is so much easier to manage than when you try to turn your back on it.

We have to be proactive in life

Hard work and a positive mind are vital for success in anything

You can listen to the episode that started it all at frankybanky.com/1

ssssssssseeeee... ssssssssseeee... sssssssseeeeeevvvvvveeenteeeeeeeeeen

Franky Banky was designed way before my stuttering epiphany. In the 1990s, a friend asked me to design a fox character for his website. I wasn't happy with the outcome so every so often, I'd try to redesign it as a fun challenge for myself.

In the early days of my podcast, I posted comics about stuttering which I created. Franky Banky was my choice as the protagonist. He seemed to be a perfect fit. Since then, I've had the feeling that a few things about this choice would haunt me. So let me set the record straight right now: there's no stuttering symbolism behind his name and the fact that he was designed with no mouth (except for a few times when I need to add a mouth in order to convey the right emotion).

The first Franky Banky comic I drew and posted was a colour version of "What's Your Name". Posting my comics online was an out of comfort zone thing for me (like publishing this book). Who knows what kind of bad comments I could potentially get! So far so good. But I was blown away when I received an email from someone in India who said he printed it out and hung it up in his cubicle at work. My comic is hanging somewhere in India! That's the power of the Internet.

however, growing up, I was bothered by stuttering jokes on TV and in the movies. I had to endure sitting right next to my friends laughing at the jokes. Not at all comfortable. When I watch those scenes today through my new perspective, I... and that some of the jokes really were funny and in jest while others were just plain wrong. At least in my opinion. I know many fellow stutterers who appreciate the jokes no matter how cruel I may interpret them to be. While I enjoy Porky Pig cartoons, others flat out do not.

What I like about Ti-Ger's design is he looks so friendly and approachable. Yes, he is supposed to be a ferocious jungle cat ready to gobble you up but he's so darn cuddly. Stuttering can suck and feel like it's devouring your chances at accomplishing anything in life however, once you put in the work and dedication required to master the tools and tips I mention throughout this book, you'll begin to embrace your stuttering, too.

OH YOU SILLY BOY! GIGGLE BY NOT HIDING HIS STUTTERING OR TRYING TO AVOID OR SWITCH WORDS OR BE IN SOME SORT OF DENIAL ABOUT HIS STUTTERING, FRANKY BANKY DIDN'T STIFLE HIMSELF OR LET HIS STUTTERING CONTROL HIM! IT WAS **HE** WHO KICKED BUTT, NOT HIS STUTTERING. AS SOON AS FRANKY BANKY LET HIS SPEECH BOSS HIM AROUND, THINGS GOT UNBEARABLE. LIKE A TIGER CHOMPING ON HIS BUTT.

How do you tame your ti-ger? That's what this book is all about! Turn the page and let's continue...

The Stuttering Toolbox

...NO, I'M STILL HERE.
I JUST ST-ST-STUTTER.
I N-N-N-N-NEED
TIME TO GET MY
W-W-WORDS—WORDS
OUT...
ANYWAY, ABOUT
THIS "SYS-SYS-SYSTEM
ACCESS FEE" ON
MY BILL...

The Wonderful World of
Desensitisation

Peace of ourselves and peace in the reaction of others. Not worrying about what others are thinking when they catch us stuttering and not worrying how we feel about "being caught". This includes cashiers, waiters, telemarketers, ticket takers, and everyone else you speak to.

After all, you can't change your body's reaction to stuttering without having peace of mind during your stuttering moments. For example, you're at a restaurant ordering some food. You're paying for the food so why should you or anyone else care how you say your order? It is the waiter's job to take your order and not ours to care if we get their approval or not.

Many speech therapies include desensitisation exercises like trips to a shopping mall to stutter openly to 100 people by asking for the time or doing a survey. Don't worry, you're usually with someone when you do it ;)

Give yourself some speaking challenges and stick to them. Something like making one phone call per day to a random store to ask what time they close. Then increase this number. Soon you will be so confident that you'll be doing this without a worry in the world.

And you will feel really good and powerful about conquering this fear!

The Benefits of
Advertising

Telling cashiers, waiters, telemarketers, ticket takers, and everyone else you speak to that you stutter. If we don't tell them, how will they know that we're ok with our stuttering?

Advertising is a part of desensitisation. And over time it also teaches us to learn to live with stuttering gracefully. What a great feeling it is to have a stutter come up, mention it, then move on.

Seriously, no one cares that we stutter. Those who matter to us anyway. Those who make a negative thing out of our stuttering, well, you have to be honest with yourself, there's something wrong with them not us. Here's a technique you can add to the desensitisation exercises you do. For instance, when you call up a store to ask what time they close, you can mention that you stutter. Say, if the person on the other end tries to finish your sentence. "You don't have to worry about finishing my sentences. I just stutter" and smile. Yes it's over the phone but smiling ensures you have a positive tone.

Activism isn't our goal here. Remember, some fluenters just don't know what to do. And people in the service industry are supposed to help their customers (or some in the restaurant industry may have been instructed by their bosses to get customers in and out of the door as quickly as possible). So naturally, they may feel they

...NO, I'M STILL HERE.
I JUST ST-ST-STUTTER.
I N-N-N-N-NEED
TIME TO GET MY
W-W-WORDS—WORDS
OUT...
ANYWAY, ABOUT
THIS "SYS-SYS-SYSTEM
ACCESS FEE" ON
MY BILL...

are helping us when they finish our sentences. No biggie. It's not you, it's them. You may also be tempted to apologise for stuttering. I went through this phase until I've finally built up the skill in advertising with ease. Now I usually advertise when I have a train wreck of a stutter or just happen to bring up my podcast or Stutter Social. Nothing wrong with apologising in a looks-like-we-just-got-interrupted-and-I-need-to-do-some-advertising sort of way, just as long as you're not *apologising* for stuttering. After all, no one expects people who use wheelchairs to apologise for using wheelchairs.

Another benefit of overt stuttering and putting yourself out there is you can also do your part in spreading stuttering awareness!

 VS.

AND THEN THIS TIGER CHOMPED MY B-B-B-B-B-B...SORRY...

AND THEN THIS TIGER CHOMPED MY B-B-B-B-B-B...HEH, STUTTERING. W-WHAT CAN YOU DO? ANYWAY, AS I WAS SAYING...

<take big breath>twenty se... ven

The Practicality of
Speech Tools

I'd like to add one more thing to my list: Speech therapy isn't a cure for stuttering. Accept it.

However and fortunately, you will learn a few methods, also known as "speech tools", that will help you control your stuttering when situations arise. Notice that I said *control* and not stop. Mastering speech tools will help you stutter gracefully instead of being caught up in a train wreck of a stutter.

Accepting and stuttering openly is great but there will be times when you'd prefer not to stutter These tools can come in handy! Keep in mind that you must stay in practice with these speech tools just like you must stay in practice with a sport. You can practice the speech tools you learned as you do your desensitization and advertising exercises.

YouTube can be your friend with samples of speech tools but you would definitely benefit from a reputable, qualified, and licensed speech pathologist who specializes in stuttering. It's like having a personal trainer. Consult your country's stuttering or speech pathology association. Or ask on a stuttering forum on a social media network. Look for posters with a good reputation, who seem to be trusted, and who

<said as fast as possible>twentyeight!

have been participating for a long time. Word of mouth is great for finding a great speech pathologist.

Warning: There are many people out there on the Internet preying on stutterers who are desperate to get rid of their stuttering. They sell stuttering "cures" but provide no research to back up their claims. Buyer beware!

As of this writing, there is no cure for stuttering (which isn't all that bad since there are many, many benefits to building a thick skin and our inner strength). Keep an eye on reputable science journals if you'd like to keep abreast of things.

How can you tell if something you've read on the Internet is shady? These sites tend to make you scroll through a long, long web page filled with large bold text, an abundance of exclamations marks, words written in caps, stock photos, and a promise of eliminating stuttering within a short time a very short time. They usually also contain a lot of quotes from "satisfied customers".

I don't mean to be a fear monger but there isn't much proof in who actually wrote those reviews. Ditto for before and after videos. They do not provide clear evidence. Colin Firth learned how to stutter on camera after all.

And most of all, if they have a big secret cure that some other person gave solely to them. This is how cults are started. Check credentials (if they don't have any, run) and consult speech pathology associations.

Hint: everything in life takes hard work and dedication. Accept it.

Hint #2: I've noticed most of these "cures" advertise NLP techniques (Neuro Linguistic Programming). These aren't cures, they are simply different ways to keep yourself thinking positively. Just like this book! Google "NLP" to learn more.

Bonus:
Voluntary Stuttering

Yup, stuttering on purpose! And yes, it is actually, totally, really, an honest-to-goodness advantage!

I've never mastered this technique, however I know many people who use it. They are in full control and ready when the real stuttering comes up. Your stuttering becomes more graceful and it is also empowering to stutter on your own terms. It helps take the pressure off, too.

My friend Greg describes it best: "For us, stuttering isn't optional. But what is optional is how we stutter. Our stuttering can either be a struggle, or it can be graceful; this is ultimately our choice. Don't get me wrong, changing how we stutter is hard work! But improvement is always possible."

My friend Evan Sherman actually enjoys voluntary stuttering. "It's so much easier to stutter voluntarily and controlled than involuntarily with so much tension. It is a way to stutter on purpose with very little tension. Its wonderful! Plus once you do it, you are no longer hiding from your stuttering. Anxiety about speaking has decreased and you now have no reason to hide your stuttering. You have already stuttered openly."

A Google search should bring up tips on getting started in voluntary stuttering.

th-th-th-th-thirty <hey, that wasn't so bad>

Secret Weapon:
Thinking Positively

We can choose how we react to our own negative thoughts. Doing a presentation and you are worried about failing? You will tank. Think positively and you will soar. This happened to me the first time I gave a presentation as part of a panel at a podcasting conference. I introduced myself, blocked big time with secondaries, started worrying, and began to do badly. Then I noticed no reaction from the audience. *"Then I may not be doing too badly"*, I thought. And I wasn't nervous for the rest of my presentation. It's common for anyone to be nervous about public speaking regardless of fluency. It is said that fluenters are more afraid of public speaking than of their own death.

I noticed that I started thinking negative thoughts whenever I looked at an audience member who had no expression on their face. But I was encouraged when I looked at an audience member with a smile on their face! Luckily, there were many smilers in the room so I only focused on them. And I was not nervous. I was joking with the audience and I actually enjoyed being up there.

Thinking positively works in all aspects of life. When you're making a call, avoid thinking *"oh please don't let me stutter please don't let me stutter"*. You'll tank because *your body will go wherever your mind takes it*. Instead, think, *"I can do this"*. Stutter and all. As you're giving your food order, try not to focus too much on whether or not the waiter approves. They are there to serve you. Thinking positively also helps you to be ready for advertising and educating should that waiter snicker or make an ignorant comment.

Keeping positive thoughts also enables us to react to our stuttering with humour. Nothing attracts people and shows confidence more than having a good sense of humour about our quirks. And I don't mean humour that puts yourself down which can be a turn off and set a negative tone for everyone.

Secret weapon:
Reading body language

Years ago I bought a book about interpreting body language. Body language consists of certain gestures, postures and even actions that we do which convey to the people we are talking to (and vice versa) our feelings, how open or closed we are to the conversation we're having and even if we like the person. *And we do these actions without realizing it.*

Upon finishing the book, I quickly learned how useful this type of knowledge was for me in thinking positively in various speaking and social situations such as job interviews, office politics and even gauging if a girl I was talking to was interested in me or not. If the body language of the other person is revealed as being positive, then there's no need to even worry about stuttering in the first place! If negative, don't automatically assume it's because of your stuttering. It could be for any other number of reasons. Knowing body language can even help you "disarm" the negative person.

I won't be able to teach you everything you need to know about body language as it's outside the scope of this book. There are lots of books out there on the subject. Consult your local bookstore. If you're interested, the book I have is entitled *The Definitive Book of Body Language* by Allan and Barbara Pease.

Secret Weapon:
Eye Contact

Maintaining eye contact is an important part of communication. It forms a connection with the people we are speaking to and shows that we are interested in what they have to say. Losing eye contact implies lying, hiding the truth, or being fearful. I know a number of people who don't stutter and never keep eye contact. To be frank, I find this incredibly irritating as it creates a distance between both parties. Plus, I'm the one working hard at keeping the habit of maintaining eye contact and they don't stutter!

When I'm speaking with a fellow stutterer who is trying to maintain eye contact, I sense more confidence and self-esteem than the non-stutterer looking elsewhere. When you stutter, your body may feel like it "needs" to shut your eyes or look way in order to push your words out. But you have to try to stay in control. Work to break the habit of looking away and good things will happen. Eye contact implies confidence and also makes us feel confident. And feeling confident makes us feel good. And feeling good is great!

Keeping eye contact may be difficult at times because stuttering can be an intimate experience between us and the people we're talking to. We can be in the middle of sharing a story or joke when suddenly we have a block. The silence formed can be awkward and can make us feel vulnerable. It can be hard to keep eye contact in that kind of moment when stuttering can make us feel naked. Perhaps the listener also loses eye contact so that we can have some privacy during our vulnerable moment?*

If you have trouble maintaining natural eye contact and feel like you're staring at the person you're talking to, try just "noticing" their eye colour. It removes the pressure off yourself and next thing you know, eye contact will come naturally to you. If the idea of looking at someone in the eye scares you, try looking around their eyes first – along their eyebrows, under the eye – then start to "notice" their eye colour. Another tip comes from actors and public speakers who practice maintaining eye contact by talking in the mirror.

I-I-I-I....
AM P-P-P-
PERFECT
FOR THE
JOB B-B-B-
BECAUSE....

VS.

I-I-I-I....
AM P-P-P-
PERFECT
FOR THE
JOB B-B-B-
BECAUSE....

*My friend and Stutter Social co-founder, Mitch Trichon, first mentioned this in a Stutter Social hangout. I think he is spot with describing the stuttering experience for both the speaker and listener.

Yet another secret weapon:
Strength training

I discovered strength training in December 2012. Basically it's lifting heavy and only doing compound lifts. I'm not going to go into the details (Google can) but the reason I'm bringing this up as a tool in your stuttering toolbox is, well, let me tell you a story...

It was March 2013 and I was just under three months into my new workout routine of focussing on building my physical strength instead of aesthetics. I was amazed at the gains I had been achieving in that short time compared to the 15+ years I've wasted doing the more popular routines people usually do. I was walking down King Street in Toronto's downtown core, heading towards a pub to meet up with some friends after a strategy brainstorm session for the Canadian Stuttering Association.

I was a few blocks away from the pub when I suddenly realized the unthinkable. I was walking with my head high and feeling confident. And *capable*. After a couple of decades with my habit of walking with my head down and avoiding eye contact with anyone, you can imagine that this was difficult not to notice!

I also realized I wasn't walking. I was *strutting*. This thought made me chuckle. This was totally not my character. That's when I realized that building your physical strength also builds your *inner strength*. Reading up on the topic, men were made to be strong. This taps into our primal days of relying on our strength to get food, build shelter, etc. For the modern man, we need to keep ourselves in shape so we can help others. Help a friend move, build a house for organizations like Habitat For Humanity, protect your family, etc. This applies to women as well.

Without keeping yourself in shape, you're only going to eventually disappoint the ones who are depending on you to help them when they need you. Or embarrass yourself as you have trouble moving furniture or injure yourself doing it.

A few months later, I was at work helping to clean up after an event. Something heavy needed to be lifted up off the floor and place it on a table. I gave it a try and to my surprise, I had no problem at all. Because of the strength training I was doing, my muscles had already been conditioned for such a task. I squatted down towards the floor (never lift with your back) put my arms around the item and lifted the heavy item off the floor. I was able to help out my colleagues and keep my fragile male ego intact.

Because of that, my colleagues know that I can be counted on to help out. Stuttering or not. It's a great feeling to help others out and a great self-confidence boost when you know you can be counted on.

Strength training has its benefits for both men and women; raised energy levels, fewer injuries when you get older, looking younger, running faster, keeping up with little ones and yes, the side benefit of looking awesome. It's only natural that people will be attracted to something that looks nice. Just don't let this go to your head. No one likes a conceited person and just like our stuttering, no one cares about our gym goals. Inner strength and a strong character are far more important qualities. Who cares if you stutter when you are a person of strong character?

If you want to give strength training a try but the idea of spending lovely summer days in a gym doesn't appeal to you, you're in luck! Strength training doesn't need to be conducted in a gym. You can use your own bodyweight. Search YouTube for exercises and sample routines.

No matter the routine or method, please check with your doctor and use proper form when doing the exercises in order to avoid injury.

Since my stuttering happens in my upper chest, my stuttering increases big time after a particularly intense workout and I'm breathing heavier for quite a while after leaving the gym.

Some coffee shops ask us for our names when we give our orders. We could look at this as a horrible ordeal or an opportunity – more chances to work on the tools in our stuttering toolbox! It's like working out in the gym and building our inner strength. Plus, baristas tend to be interested in getting to know their customers. Win-win.

The caffeine in coffee seems to increase my stuttering. Actually, I can't help but to chuckle at how fast my stuttering increases right after drinking a cup.

In spite of this, there are situations where I feel it's best to reduce my chances of stuttering uncontrollably such as job interviews, which is a topic I'll get to shortly.

In job interviews (well, all speaking situations), I am aware that I can never truly know what the interviewer may be thinking with regards to my stuttering regardless of how many tools or secret weapons I use from the stuttering toolbox. So while I can't magically eliminate my stuttering, I can prevent the effects of caffeine jitters.

thirty sssssssssssssssssssssssss<six?>ssssssssseven<oh!>

Another tool in the box:
Build A Support System

The most important tool in the stutterer's toolbox, in my opinion, is having a support system. Be it online and/or offline. This book wouldn't exist if I didn't have a support system. Spending time with people who share our unique experiences helps us feel less alone on both our "good" and "bad" speech days.

We also learn from each other, too. Mentors are awesome. They've been where we are, pass their wisdom onto us as we are motivated by their confidence.

Having a support system also enables you to help others. In addition, helping others comes with its own set of benefits including allowing us to grow by developing ourselves as leaders, mentors and, well, it puts all of our life's challenges into perspective.

Consider making the effort to attend a stuttering support group in your area if there is one. Online groups like Stutter Social and stuttering forums on social networks are great but us humans are social beings. We need in-person contact.

Maybe a few of you can do desensitisation and advertising exercises together at malls and such. There is nothing more enjoyable than helping each other win.

If there isn't a support group in your area, would you be up for starting one? A Google search should bring up tips and best practices.

<big breath>thir<big breath>ty<big breath>eight

My friend Greg and I created a thriving stuttering community in the early days of Twitter. We had a lot of fun making friends with fellow stutterers and SLPs all over the world and helping each other out with the stuttering toolbox, encouraging others to take the baby steps in building the nerve

to make phone calls, preparing for job interviews, sharing our wins and losses, and regular off topic stuff.

I was able to share my joy with my friends on Twitter right after I aced my first solo presentation at a digital conference. It felt great to share that milestone with friends who fully understood and lived the stuttering experience just like I did.

The Twitter community vibe was positive. Everyone was willing to give being proactive a try. There were no trolls. A few of my friends appeared on my podcast and I even got to meet a few of them in person!

That's the beauty of social media and our digital gadgets. It helps to form relationships which solidify when we eventually meet in person. Our friends are reachable in an asynchronous way transcending time zones.

I wrote an ebook about this back in 2009. It has a rather lengthy title of *YOU have the awesome ability to make positive changes to the lives of people all over the world via personal interaction through podcasts (and other social media tools)*.

You can download it for free at frankybanky.com/2.

th-th-th-thirty n-n-n-n-n-n-n-nine

And another tool in the box:
Pursue your interests and get yourself out there

Life doesn't stop happening just because you stutter (have I made myself clear?). As you pursue your interests and put yourself out there, you will come to realize and experience that no one truly cares that we stutter. They only care about the person inside of us. Really!

If you're friendly, people will like you. If you're not, they won't. And vice versa. Simple as that. The anger you may feel towards yourself because of your stuttering will actually end up pushing people away.

Pursuing your interests will also create opportunities you will never imagine. For instance, take my interest in podcasting. I was able to work on desensitisation, advertising, and a few speech tools while I attended meet ups and conferences.

It all started in early 2007 for me when I ventured out to my first conference. It was about podcasting. I would have never, ever imagined that over the next few years I'd make numerous new friends, speak at and co-organize conferences, and be featured in the newspaper, on the radio, and on national TV! I picked up new skills which also helped me find my current job and be asked to co-found Stutter Social. All this wouldn't have happened if I had stayed home and kept my mouth shut back in 2007.

Sure it was scary to talk to strangers and embarrassing to get "the look", but I couldn't have grown without experiencing them. Advertising and educating eliminated the looks. Experiencing the pain and embarrassment of train wreck stuttering and funny looks is the only way you can learning from "failure" and grow.

Toddlers repeatedly fall down when they learn how to walk. Yet they unconditionally try and try again until it comes naturally to them. You have to get yourself into a gym and go through the pain of exercise if you want to become stronger.

And no one is going to know how good and normal you really are if you don't give them a chance to hear the words you have to say or get to know you. Unfortunately for us, that requires repeated feats of courage (not bad at all, really!) and advertising our stuttering.

You have to be a self-promoter so don't hide. Get out there and talk to people. Getting ourselves into as many speaking situations as we can is like — altogether now — going to the gym. We're building our inner strength.

By the way, all those people who gave me funny looks at my first taste of networking back in 2007 — we're all good friends now.

I was actually nervous about attending my first stuttering conference! If I hadn't gone, I don't think I would have met so many cool new friends who would further inspire me.

SOMETiME DURiNG 2008 OR 2009

A bunch of us went to grab a bite to eat at a nearby pub after our toastmasters for people who stutter meeting. We were looking at our menus and having small talk when quite out of the blue, it hit me. Everyone at the table stutters just like me. And just like me they will have to endure stuttering through their orders. I was hanging out with friends who stuttered just like me.

BAR-BAR-BAR
BE-BE-BE-BE-
CUE-CUE-CUE-
CHICKEN SALAD

S-S-S-
S-S-S-
SLIVERS
FOR
M-M-ME

Ch-ch-ch-
CHEEEESE
b-b-b-b-
burger —

Ch-Ch-Ch-
Ch-Ch-Ch-
Chicken
f-f-f-f...

C-CLLLL-
CLUB
SSSSSS...
SAND-
WICH

The whole world suddenly seemed brighter. Stuttering our orders became thrilling. I was no longer the only one at the table with the unique experience of stuttering and nobody else understanding.

Throughout our meal we were stuttering, joking, talking about our day jobs, laughing and stuttering some more.

Mind you, a few at our table weren't too thrilled about stuttering but for me it was great feeling of belonging.

I felt this way again when I went to my 1st stuttering conference. It was held by the National Stuttering Association (NSA) and that year, 2010, it took place in Cleveland, Ohio.

There must have been about 600 of us among families and speech language pathologists. We filled up a huge, huge hotel in downtown Cleveland.

I remember standing in the middle of the crowd right after registering and thinking to myself "stuttering is the norm here!" **IT BLEW MY MIND**

THE general assembly was packed. Speakers made side jokes about their stuttering, kids shared their stories. Again, the world seemed to be a little brighter.

BEING Among hundreds of other stuttering adults made making friends really easy. And stuttering even created a few new social cues and etiquette.

For example, when you meet someone in the "real world", you shake their hand, tell them your name, and let go of their hand.

when you meet someone at a stuttering conference, you shake hands and... I still am not sure what to do.

Hi! I'M F-F-F-F-F-F-F-F-F-F-FRRRANKY B-B-BANKY.

P-P-P-P-P-P-P.....P...P...PLEA...PLEASED...T-T-T-To M-M-M...

MEET YOU. I...I...I...I...I...I...I...I...I...I... I...I...I...I...

WE'RE STILL HOLDING HANDS

WE'RE STILL HOLDING HANDS

A) You continue holding each other's hands, until the two of you have finished saying your names. And this can take a good while which is also awkward in the "real world".

I...I...I...AM-AM..B...B...B...B

WHEN DO WE LET GO?

B—

IF I LET GO, IT'S RUDE

B—

B...B....B—

Bil-l-l-l-Bilo-Bilo...Bilodo.

Whew!

WHEW!

B) You let go while the other person is stuttering his/her name. But this can be rude and imply impatience.

Hi! I'M F-F-FF-F-F-F-F-F-FRRRANKY B-B-BANKY

P-P-P-P-P-P..P...P...PLEA...PLEASED...T-T-T-To M-M-M...

MEET YOU. I...I...I...I...I...I...I...I...I...I...I...

I always felt awkward with option A. And I can sense the other person feeling the same way.
And I always felt rude with option B.

fourty three <I felt a stutter coming on but it didn't end up happening>

I made some great friends and enjoyed hearing each other stutter not just openly but so freely. "This is how I was made to talk", I thought to myself. No fighting, no energy spent on trying to control my communication disorder, I was being 100% ME.

S-S-SAY CH-CH-CH-CHEESE!

CH-CH-CH CHEESE! HA HA HA HA HA HA

And I had no choice but to stutter openly at bars and in restaurants. With all that stutter comaraderie, why bother to avoid and switch words?

I was among good company and we chuckled at the look of wonder restaurant staff would sometimes have as everyone at their table — and most times the entire establishment! — gave their orders with bumpy speech. This is always a highlight for me.

HEE HEE HEE HEE HEE

UM?

You should definitely check out any upcoming Stuttering conferences. I can highly recommend the NSA conference as it's a positive and supportive community.

And a lot of fun!

You return home with new energy and motivation to stutter freely or give advertising a try.

St-St-Stuttering is c-c-c-cool, YEAH!

WELCOME BACK TO CANADA. DO YOU HAVE ANYTHING TO DECLARE?

I think this book wouldn't exist if I had never attended an NSA conference. This is why you need to hang out with other people who stutter. Better if they are positive about their stuttering. Us humans do better when we get help from our friends. For some reason, us humans tend to think we can handle life on our own. But we're social beings. We learn from our mentors and we get inspired by each other's stories.

f-f-f-f-f-f-f-f-f-f-f-f-f-f-fourty f-f-f-f-f-f-f-f-f-f-f-f-f-f-f-four

I feel for those who stutter who aren't comfortable among others who stutter and not willing to get out of their comfort zone. They are missing out on a lot of motivation and the opportunity to unlock their perceived limitations.

If you do check out a stuttering conference, or any kind of conference really, you get what you put into it. It may seem like there are cliques but that's only because old friendships have been made and they are simply catching up from the previous year or so. They will be open to making new friends. But you also have to put in the effort. Look for others who may be alone or maybe even volunteer.

Or do what I did — produce a podcast about stuttering and interview everyone for an episode! You can hear all about my experiences at my first conference at frankybanky.com/4.

If you'd like to see what an NSA conference looks like, I also shot video episodes in the proceeding years. Search for "Stuttering is Cool" on YouTube (or go to frankybanky.com/5).

To quote David Seidler, the screenwriter of The King's Speech, who gave a fantastically inspiring keynote at the NSA conference in 2011;

> *"If you can live through a childhood of stuttering, you can live through anything.*
>
> *And if you go into adulthood still stuttering, you can handle anything...*
>
> *You have been tempered by the fire."*

Yet another tool in the box:
Have a creative outlet

Expressing yourself when you stutter can be quite challenging when the people around you are talking at a much faster rate. We live in a fast-paced world which generally does not understand that those of us who stutter need some extra time to say what we need to say. An unfortunate consequence is our peers don't get a chance to get to know us. Having a creative outlet can be quite therapeutic and can connect us with others.

Creative expression is often dismissed as unimportant or being a frivolous activity. Arts programs lose their funding, focus in schools is placed on other endeavors like sports and math. Don't get me wrong, these are important in life, I'm just saying that creative expression — be it visual art, photography, making music, singing, writing, dancing, wood working, restoring a vintage motorcycle — and having your creativity nurtured comes with a lot of untapped benefits.

Drawing comics is an activity I enjoyed since I was a little kid reading *Peanuts*. I was a big fan of newspaper comics and always felt good after scribbling out a story that I thought was funny or when I dabbled in what I termed "cartoon fine art"*. It was a great way to show the world something that I created myself with my own hands. Be it a joke I thought up, a particular cartoon character I designed or, later, a website I put together.

I had an epiphany when I started my new job at a rehabilitation hospital for children with disabilities which has an active arts program. Children with a variety of abilities and communication disorders are able to communicate with the world through the hobbies they enjoy despite whatever limitations their disabilities may challenge them with.

Expressing ourselves creatively also gives us the freedom to try new things (another form of getting out of our comfort

*Fine art, cartoon style. My mediums are pencil, ink, and oil pastel. I've dabbled with acrylic paint but I'm not quite dexterous with brushes. Yet.

zones), make mistakes and try something that wasn't made by anyone else before. It gives us a sense of pride in our work, our creation, and a feeling of accomplishment at telling a story. Creative expression can also help us with self-discovery. Creative expression is a better alternative to mind numbing stuff like TV, excessive Facebooking, drinking, drugs, and emotional eating. Instead, you can be productive and tap into your vocation, your calling. Maybe even write a book about stuttering, or a blog, podcast, maybe record an album of music?

There are also many health benefits to creative expression. I read about studies of seniors who stay creative remain healthier longer, had fewer hopsital visits, used fewer medications, had higher morale, and were more socially active, less lonely, and more optimistic.

Unfortunately, the opportunity to creatively express ourselves decreases and vanishes as we grow into adults. As described in Hugh MacLeod's *Creative Manifesto**, "we are given a box of crayons on our first day of school as kids. We lose those crayons as adults as we toil away in our day jobs. At one point, our soul gets tired and craves something fulfilling and creative and asks for the box of crayons back".

Try to fit some regular time to nurture your creative side. You will feel great and by connecting this way with others, you may also inspire them.

*You can download this free ebook at frankybanky.com/3

This is the first illustration I made of Franky Banky that I mentioned a few pages back. I was noodling around with some markers when he suddenly appeared and took form.

Now let me share with you some advice for managing your stuttering in certain speaking situations...

f-fourty s-seven

The telephone

Once you explain that you stutter and need time to get the words out, the party at the other end will give you all the time in the world to speak. Remember, some people just need educating for whatever reason. Some people are just plain jerks, too, and their reaction is never a reflection of you. It is their problem that they are jerks. Focus on the positive people in your life.

You can disclose at the beginning of the call or wait until a nice, big, juicy stutter comes out. You can simply say "I stutter" and if you like, add "I need some extra time to speak". No big deal. Stuttering should never be a big, horrible secret. A technique I use to control and minimize stuttering when I'm about to make a phone call is I plan out what I need to say and keep thinking positively throughout the call. Don't write an actual script or else they will know you are reading.

If you feel otherwise, you can use a method radio announcers use to not sound like they are reading. Write out what you need to say but only use up under half the width of the page. I find that keeping each line about 60 characters long is good.

Check out episode 99 of Stuttering is Cool where I interview a friend (who makes an appearance in the Rent-A-Cute-Puppy comic coming up) who shares her tips on surviving phone calls; frankybanky.com/6.

FORTUNATELY MY SPEECH IS SHORT

HOWEVER, S-S-SINCE I S-S-STUTTER, WE L-L-WON'T REALLY B-BB-BE SAVING MUCH TIME ANYWAY

Public speaking

My friend Jonathon began his best man speech with "Even though I stutter, I wanted to give this speech for my friend on his special day". He received an enthusiastic applause and warm compliments by many of the wedding guests afterwards. Nobody laughed at him.

I was nervous before I gave my first presentation at a job years ago. But a few moments before I began, I realized that I speak to my colleagues one on one every day. Giving a presentation at work is no different. All my colleagues needed to know was the information that I knew. These positive thoughts helped me stay calm and give a smooth presentation. Yeah I stuttered, but I was still able to communicate. It can be hard to stay positive while public speaking. I began to tank whenever a negative thought came into my head. And I rescued myself by thinking positively again.

It's up to you to gauge if disclosing is comfortable or appropriate for the type of presentation you're giving. Yes, certain situations do not call for advertising but when you do, disclose gracefully and with a smile. Adding some humour always helps – "You might have noticed that I'm stumbling on my words. I stutter." Maybe throw in a joke like "I'd like to think it has something to do with standing in front of 700 people but that is not the case". Then move on.

Again, your audience will only care about what you have to say and not how you say it. But you had better know your stuff because that will put you at ease. Otherwise, you will be nervous and start off the negative thinking spiral and tank. Practice your presentation until you know it 100%.

I stutter. Don't panic.

Grant Meredith, a friend of mine, says this every time he begins a speech in front of a new group or new class at the university where he lectures.

He uses humour to put everyone at ease and carries on.

As I mentioned earlier, when I give a speech or presentation, I try not to worry about the the nondescript or unhappy faces in the audience. My worries dissipate whenever I look at someone with a smiling face. It means they are fully engaged with my presentation. And no, they were not laughing at my stuttering.

I felt an impending sense of doom every time the phone rang as I grew up. It would get worse when it turned out to be a long distance call. That meant it was an Italian-speaking relative from Italy or USA. Some who stutter speaking other languages fluently. Not me. I had to think about not stuttering and remember my Italian vocabulary. In fact, I came up with my own avoidance tricks for that. Both types of avoidance put a huge damper on these calls despite how much I enjoyed talking to my relatives. You'd think I'd have taken the time to learn the language but instead I chose to pretend that I didn't know how to say a particular word in Italian.

MEANWHILE, AT A COMPLETELY UNRELATED EVENT ACROSS TOWN, SOME CHILDREN ARE ALL A-BUZZ WITH EXCITING NEWS...

BILLY GOT A PUPPY!!

HE DID? LET'S GO SEE!

HIS N-N-N-NAME IS CH-CH-CHESTNUT

HE'S SO CUTE!

OOO!

AHHH!

AhhH!

OOO!

END

@ Davide Rossi.ca

Inspired by the military, I came up with an idea for a punishment for using avoidance techniques. Every time you avoid, drop and do 20 push ups. I once owed myself 75 of them after only an hour or so. Yes, I did them.

Dating

Does she or he see past your stuttering?

NO → Plenty of other fish in the sea

Yes ↓

Great!

SUAVE

Dating is a challenging and stressful thing for everybody regardless of speech. If the person who you're interested in can't see past your stuttering, then they aren't worth your time no matter how hot they are. Accept it. Plenty of other fish in the sea.

And I think it's best not to hide your stuttering from the person whom you're dating. I've met people who do that and they never grow out of their comfort zones. They continue trying to play this game of hiding the stutter from their significant other and eventually, spouse. I don't know how they are able to consider their relationship a strong one with such a lack of trust in themselves or their spouse. A successful relationship involves two people. Not one.

Advertising your stuttering to new people can be quite a challenge. I simply wait for either a train wreck to come up — hey, I can't help it if I let my stuttering work for me — or when they ask what I did over the weekend.

If the latter, that's when I can mention working on my podcast or hosting Stutter Social ("*I saw the sun rise in India during a hangout!*"). Or travelled somewhere for a stuttering conference. You'd be amazed at how much fluenters are interested in learning about stuttering and our conferences.

I've heard of a guy who strikes up conversation with women in bars by asking if they would mind chatting so he could practice his speech tools. Apparently he got a lot of dates that way! Yup, that's where that comic on page 28 came from. You can even try this little trick with online dating when things move on from the website to the first or second date.

Stuttering is our advantage as it's a social filter. If your date doesn't like your stuttering, then you know he or she isn't your type. Feel free to disclose right in your profile if you're comfortable but remember dating is like a job interview. Speaking of which...

That person won't make a good boss or colleague

Does the interviewer see past your stuttering?

No →

Yes ↓

Great!

Job interviews are all about revealing your past behaviours to the potential employer. They won't necessarily care about your stuttering. If they do, they aren't the employer for you. It will only be a bad work environment.

Your mission in a job interview is to put yourself in a positive light as you reveal your behaviors in the past. And it is the employer's mission to figure out all the reasons why they shouldn't hire you. This has nothing to do with speech. They do this with each and every applicant. You need to show in all your answers how, as part of your professional experience, you solved the problems of your clients, customers, superiors and co-workers, how you benefitted your team and achieved what your manager needed you to do.

If you have a stuttering-related answer, make sure it's relevant to the job you're interviewing for. This way you can also show how your stuttering has never been an issue even without the employer having to ask regardless if they are wondering. See? Stuttering gives us opportunities to let our stuttering work for us. I wait until an unexpected train wreck of a stutter erupts and use that as the opportunity to disclose. I smile and say "I also stutter" and include examples of how my stuttering never affected my job performance in my answers to the employer's questions without actually mentioning my stuttering. For instance, scenarios involving interaction with clients and colleagues. By simply talking about how I excelled in these kinds of scenarios, who cares how I talked?

I share a ton of job search tips for the 21st century on episode 147 of Stuttering is Cool. Check them out at frankybanky.com/7.

Just like with dating, you want to appear confident in your stuttering. Fluenters take cues on how to react to our stuttering from us. If we look to be at ease with our stuttering, they will feel we are at ease and confident. If potential employers sense that you feel your stuttering is a negative issue, chances are they may not want to hire you.

Should you include stuttering in your resume and/or cover letter? Only if it is relevant to the position is my advice. You can mention that you regularly attend Toastmasters (if you do). Mention what you do if you're active in the stuttering community. Especially if you lead a support group. *Employers love leaders.* Remember, they only care what you can do for them.

Try not to waste any energy on worrying that stuttering won't get you a job. I know telemarketers, teachers, lawyers, soldiers, astronomers, engineers, journalists, and lecturers who stutter. And should you not end up getting a job (it's pretty rare for anyone to get a job after just one application process), don't assume it's because of your stuttering. It's a challenge for anyone of all speech fluency levels to land a job.

Job search these days is all about *who knows you*. And if no one knows you, then you'll need to be proactive and meet people in your target industry. It's no longer about blindly sending volumes of resumes and cover letters to job ads. We have to get out there and meet people.

Speaking of which...

Networking

Networking can take place at a conference, a meet up, a party, anywhere. And it can be intimidating for anybody to strike up a conversation with strangers. But it doesn't have to be scary. Use your stuttering toolbox to your advantage!

I will share seven tips I picked up as I bumbled my way towards learning how to network.

1. Go with someone who is great at networking. In 2007, I was fortunate to have my brother-in-law with me my first time networking. He's stellar at schmoozing. I observed what he did and how he simply walked up to someone and said "Hello my name is...". Such a simple phrase to say yet so difficult for us stutterers to say it. Later, we split up so we could do our own networking. No need to turn your friend into a crutch. You can only learn from *doing*. Yes, I failed miserably a few times but *remember the toddlers!* I had some wins and some "fails", funny looks, and such, but it took me a few more networking events and meet ups to get into practice. *Networking is a skill you learn through trial and error.*

2. Use canned material. This way you don't blank out on what to say. "Is this your first time attending this event?", "Hi there! My name is....", "What brings you to attend this meet up?", "What do you do?", "What do you think about...." and mention a current event relevant to the industry. Resist the urge to play with your mobile phone. You will not be approachable as long as your eyes are looking down at a gadget.

3. Look for someone else who is alone. Chances are, they will be as self-conscious as you are and grateful that someone walked up to them.

4. Use social networks to get to know others who will be attending. Social tools such as Twitter, connect people online. Relationships form and then we tend to eventually meet in person. In other words, you will be able to tweet at someone "I look forward to finally meeting you at... Wanna do lunch?".

5. Give yourself a time limit if you are really, really self-conscious about going alone. "I'll be there for the presentation and speak to one person". You don't have to be a networking star the first time around.

6. Bring props. If it's a conference, bring a power bar, phone charger, that dongle presenters need to hook their devices to the projector. It's a great way to get noticed without having to approach anyone. You'll simply be saving someone's day by coming prepared!

7. Present. You will not only be able to introduce yourself in front of everyone all at once, but you will also be promoting yourself as a subject matter expert. I've interviewed many lecturers, teachers, professors, and presenters who stutter on my podcast. And they all report the same thing — audience members are more attentive because they are curious to hear your expert words that are being said. They don't care how.

You will find that your stuttering comes with many advantages as you put yourself out there. You just have to give it a try. These are some of the methods which worked for me. Google is your friend when searching for more networking survival tips.

Stuff fluenters say

Some people may not understand or even recognize stuttering. Though embarrassing, being asked if we forgot our name isn't the end of the world. All it takes is a short explanation and life goes on. Otherwise, the uninformed will draw their own conclusions. Like we're stupid, nervous, drunk, on drugs, or incapable of remembering our own names. *Seriously, some people may actually think we forgot our own names!* And we're supposed to be the unintelligent ones?

Little kids are curious by nature and they look to us grown ups to learn about the world. So there is no need to feel awkward when they ask us why we "talk like that". As a camp counselor, my friend Greg would get questions from kids asking why he stuttered. He'd ask them why their hair was (insert color here). The kids would shrug their shoulders, then so would Greg, and almost always, that would be the end of that.

Some people may simply be nervous when we stutter because they may not know how to react. They may not even recognize stuttering and may be wondering if we are ok. They may also wonder if it's rude to even ask us about stuttering or what is going on.

I had a good dose of what it's like to be on the other side of the stuttering the first time I met other stutterers. I was checking out a Toastmasters group for people who stutter and as soon as I started having conversations with everyone after I walked in, I realized I suddenly had egg on my face.

After many years of complaining about getting funny looks from people whenever I spoke... it was suddenly easy to forgive them. It freaked me out a bit that I didn't know what to do! After all, I do stutter myself so I should be an expert at this, right?

I was *extremely* mindful of my body language and my eyes hurt from being too conscientious to allow myself to blink.

But I made @#$% sure that I did not have any funny looks on my face!

Using humour can also help lighten the mood. Don't be afraid to laugh at yourself and make a few jokes in jest. A little bit of deprecating humour is ok and can be quite effective at making people laugh with you. But don't overdo it or else you will risk coming across as someone who is whining.

Telling fluenters not to finish your sentences I know fluenters mean well but my biggest pet peeve is when someone attempts to finish my sentences. Then I have to halt the conversation in order to explain that finishing my sentences isn't necessary. I make sure I educate with a smile so I don't come across as sounding sharp. See why we need to do our part in spreading awareness?

During my first year of high school, my sister told me about a friend's sister who stopped stuttering by placing pebbles in her mouth. I actually gave it a try! I was safety conscious enough about the risk of swallowing pebbles, so I used dried chickpeas. There I was speaking in English class with dried chickpeas sticking to the insides of my cheeks, dislodging them was unpleasant, and I kept eating them.

EXCUSE ME.
YOUR FLY
IS OPEN.

Small talk and

how to enter into a conversation

when there aren't a lot of pauses

and people are speaking too fast

Unfortunately, there isn't much we can do except for using hand gestures to signal when you'd like to speak. Maintaining eye contact also helps to get the message across that you'd like to contribute. As mentioned in the eye contact section, looking into the other person's eyes (or group of people) creates a connection.

Please try to avoid blaming your stuttering if your friends aren't attentive enough to notice that you're trying to speak and give you a chance to get a word in edgewise.

What if you're in a meeting at work and the room is full of alpha people talking a mile a minute? I found raising a hand to signal that you'd like to speak can be effective. But there's nothing much we can do if, say, you're stuck dealing with someone who's too alpha and just won't let others talk.

This is when I start to be strategic. "Excuse me, I just wanted to go back to when we talked about X and mention....". Remember when I said that employers love leaders? Well, this is one form of taking leadership. Work with what you have to deal with and make sure you make your contribution. The last thing you need is to be told by your boss that you don't contribute in meetings.

Walk into your workplace with the attitude of not letting your stuttering get in the way of your job performance. Keep your Ti-Ger on its leash.

Trying to tell a joke when you stutter can be one of the most frustrating situations in our lives. I always enjoyed sharing jokes and funny stories with friends, family and colleagues but my stuttering would always ruin the punch line.

A few of my good friends are comedians who stutter so I asked them for their advice during a special YouTube broadcast of Stutter Social where I invited Jody Fuller and Nina G. What they shared was simply, well, simple:

Practice your material

Nina G explained that punchlines are like saying our names. "There's no way of getting around them so we will stutter on them more. And that's where practising a lot lets me get to know the material very well so the pressure isn't there to get it out just right."

Just like preparing for a job interview, practice your material beforehand. This way you can gague which words are the bumpy ones and practice speech tools to use on them.

Ad lib

Jody shared that he works any unexpected stuttering into the joke he is telling. I like this idea because this makes the joke even funnier and this will also let the people you are talking to know that you are at ease with your stuttering.

Enjoy creating suspence

As I said before, needing to take some more time to get your words out can keep your listeners more engaged. They want to know what you are going to say next*.

*Just as long as they don't try to finish your sentences and ruin the punch line!

As I've mentioned many times throughout this book, there are both good and bad people on the planet. And then there are those who are complete jerks. Something happened to them in their life that made them so insecure that they need to feel like they are better than everyone else by making others feel bad. Bullies will continue to pick on you as long as they know it bothers you.

My little buddy, Nate Rogers, said it best in a YouTube video he posted when he was 11 years old about his experiences of being bullied. When bullies mimic his stuttering, Nate shares "My usual response is 'Hey could you not mock me? I stutter and sometimes it takes a little bit to get my words out. And it's kind of hurtful'. But if they do it over and over again, I'll go to the teacher or the councillor at our school. Or if it's not at school, then my parents which will definitely take care of the matter!"

"As people laugh at me because of my stutter and call me dumb, my response is usually 'So what, I stutter? And I'm not dumb.'"

It sucks to be bullied. Please remember there isn't anything wrong with you; it isn't your fault and you are still a great person; there are many other people who like you and your stuttering so you should focus on them. I know it seems like a long time from now but *it will get better as you get older.*

9 types of stutterers

A list I co-wrote with my fellow stuttering friends, Samuel Dunsiger and Evan Sherman. It is healthy to laugh at ourselves.

The Cure Chaser

They try every technique in the book, call them cures, but stutter anyway. Then try another cure the following week. They scrutinized the techniques in *The King's Speech* including finding willing participants to sit on their stomachs.

The Confident Stutterer

Always makes fluent people feel awkward by overtly stuttering on purpose. The confident stutterer makes all the phone calls, ticket orders, and is the wingman in nightclubs.

The Master of Avoidance

They're impossible to reach on the phone, easy via texting. Covert and having practically memorized both the dictionary

and thesaurus, they are able to avoid, switch words, and order food they don't want to eat. Don't ask them to order pizza for you because you will end up with Chinese takeout instead.

The Activist

Lives for stuttering awareness and always seeks out negative representations of stuttering in the media so they can shut down every TV show that mentions stuttering. They will not see the humour in this list at all.

The Overzealous Stutterer

 Tells everyone how awesome stuttering is no matter the time or place — even in a public washroom — to the puzzlement of the Cure Chaser and Master of Avoidance. They also own at least three separate websites about stuttering and moderates stuttering communities across, at minimum, four social networks. They have t-shirts printed and only date speech language pathologists.

The Stutterer-Turned-SLP

The super hero of the stuttering community. Pent up on helping others who stutter, they're dedicated to saving the world one stutterer at a time.
Unfortunately, no one on this list likes hanging out with them as they continuously advocate voluntary stuttering.

The Stutter Radar

 Listens intently to the speech patterns of all celebrities in anticipation of being the first to discover another famous person who stutters.

The Apathetic Stutterer

They don't care about their stuttering nor this list. They live their lives regardless much to the astonishment of everyone else listed here. As the ninja of the stuttering community, they are only seen once at a meet up.

The Angry Stutterer

 They blame everything on their stuttering, including climate change. They want to punch the overzealous stutterer in the face.

Keep using your stuttering toolbox

There are things that we can and cannot control. Stuttering is not your fault nor anyone else's. Nor is it a limitation. Your life will amount to something — but only if you are proactive at trying to prevent your stuttering from limiting you.

Becoming comfortable with your stuttering will take some time. It requires working on the mental energy it takes to accept and learn from failure — first. Your heart and emotional energy will follow. Wherever your head goes (thinking positively, etc.), your heart will follow. It will suck the other way around when emotions come first.

No skills for anything in life will take a few seconds to master. You will fail and you will succeed. As I've mentioned many times throughout this book, failure is not bad (just like stuttering isn't bad. Accept it.). Failure is a benefit because it's the only way we can learn. *Remember the toddlers!*

Like everything in life, mastering the tools in your stuttering toolbox requires ongoing practice. Once you stop, you will go back to avoiding and losing your sense of self-confidence. So keep practicing those speech tools, keep getting out of your comfort zone, and regularly put yourself into as many speaking situations as you can.

I urge you to stay proactive. It's all about taking risks and we can only grow from taking risks. You will have setbacks, you will experience moments where you just want to be covert. And that's ok. You're only human. But don't be covert too often. Get right back up and be proactive again. And keep in touch with your support system.

You are the only one in charge of making positive changes in your life. If you want a better life, make it happen!

If you decide to try my plethora of advice — yay! — be sure to allow your loved ones to accompany you along your journey towards stuttering confidently. Otherwise, from their point of view, suddenly one day you might become a completely different person from the brother, sister, mother, father, friend, son, daughter, etc. who they have always known. That can be quite startling for them regardless of how happy they will be for you. This doesn't necessarily mean it will be a bad thing but it is always good to share your journey with the people close to you. They want to be part of your successes!

A workshop from my first NSA conference in 2010 about this topic still resonates with me today. It was presented by my friend, Pamela Mertz, the Stutter Rock Star, who, a few months earlier, launched her podcast, *Women Who Stutter: Our Stories*. I first met Pam online in our Twitter community. In fact, it was our mutual friend Greg who gave her the stutter rockstar moniker.

Pam's workshop blew me away. She shared her story of making the decision to end a 20-year relationship with a man who ended up not having been able to adjust to the new confident and overt stuttering Pam.

Pam discovered the NSA and its supportive community in 2006 where her journey from the shy, quiet Pam who let others do the talking for her soon began. Over the next three years, Pam worked to gain confidence from being inspired to own her stuttering and make room for it (which became the name and theme of her blog).

However, Pam's boyfriend didn't grow along with her as she developed into a confident person. She wasn't the same Pam he knew and recognized. He preferred the quiet Pam who didn't own the ground she stood upon. And that wasn't the type of relationship Pam wanted anymore.

So after twenty years, Pam made the difficult decision to leave him.

Pam's story made me realize that I had unintentionally done the same thing with my family and friends. While the relationship I have with my loved ones has always been fine, Pam's workshop made me realize that I must have surprised everyone when out of the blue one day I began talking about giving presentations at digital conferences and talking about stuttering on national radio and TV. I realized then that it must have seemed quite sudden that I'd started podcasting about something I had pretty much kept quiet about all my life. Then I was interviewed in a few newspapers.

Oops.

My relationship with my friends and family wasn't at all affected by these events. I just think I might have unintentionally shocked them a little as I was always the shy and reserved type.

And Pam's doing great, too. She is a Distinguished Toastmaster (DTM) and mentor in Toastmasters and is involved with FRIENDS (The National Association of Young People Who Stutter) and the NSA.

See why you shouldn't bother with those who can't see past your stuttering and appreciate the person you are?

The end

WHAT's YOUR NAME?

PART 2

by Daniele Rossi

F-F-F-F-F-F

FR-FR-FR

FRRRA-FRRAA

AANN-NN...

K-K-K-K-K

...AAAANKy...

B-B-B-B-B

A-A-A-A-A

N-N-N-N...

KKy.

AND I STUTTER.

END ©DanieleRossi.ca

Always remember:

You can still be an effective communicator in spite of stuttering.

It's what you say that's important, not how you say it.

STUTTERINGISCOOL.COM

Fun fact: You might have noticed that Franky Banky's fur is black on the front and back covers, and on this page while his fur is white throughout the rest of the book. When I first wrote and drew this book in 2013, I made the decision to draw Franky Banky's fur white to reflect the fact that he is orange in colour (with brown arms, feet, and a white patch on his chest and on the tip of his tail).

However, a while after publishing my book, I realized that Franky Banky looked better with his fur rendered in black since I almost exclusively drew comics in black and white. So I continued colouring his fur in black. This, of course, created a little dilemma for me when I had decided to create a new cover for the French version of my book (to also use for my original English version, that you are now reading, going forward). Do I redraw all the internal comics to reflect the new black fur? Naaahhhh. I liked the idea of keeping the "classic" Franky Banky look for sentimental and historical reasons.

It's still the same Franky Banky. He's only wearing a different coat :)